Let's Be Friends

Growing Friendships

Reggie Harper

SOCIAL AND EMOTIONAL LEARNING FOR THE REAL WORLD™

Rosen Classroom™

Let's be friends!
What do friends do?

Friends smile.
They say hello.

Friends talk.
They tell stori

Friends listen.
They ask questions

Friends share.
They take turns.

Friends have fun!
They laugh and play.

Words to Know

friends

laugh

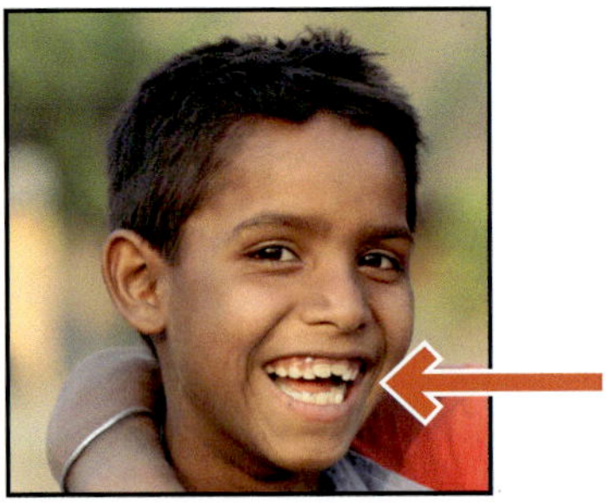

smile